On the Trail of

Colorado

Critters

Wildlife-Watching for Kids

Written by Mary Taylor Young
Photography by Wendy Shattil and Bob Rozinski

Denver Museum of Natural History

kids
WESTCLIFFE PUBLISHERS

To all Colorado critters—they enliven our world and bring us joy—and to all kids who may use this book and come to love Colorado's outdoors and its wildlife as much as we do.—MTY, WS, and BR

Many thanks to Wendy, the project team, and Sally Taylor.—MTY

Many Coloradans who share our love of wildlife have been generous with their knowledge. We thank them all. Special thanks goes to Forrest and Judy Beckman, whose support allowed us to pursue our goals.—WS and BR

This publication was supported by a generous grant from the John G. Duncan Charitable Trust, Wells Fargo Bank, Trustee.

Text © 2000 by Mary Taylor Young
Photographs © 2000 by Wendy Shattil/Bob Rozinski
Map and design © 2000 by Denver Museum of Natural History
All rights reserved.

Chapter icon silhouettes courtesy of Dorothy Emerling

DMNH project team
Project manager: Heidi M. Lumberg; Editor: James T. Alton; Designer: Jill Soukup; Proofreader: Pamela Wineman; Scientific reviewers: Cheri A. Jones, Ph.D., Curator of Mammalogy, and Kirstie M. Bay, Bouslog Fellow in Ornithology; Educational reviewer: Laurie Roulston, Life Sciences Educator

Published by Denver Museum of Natural History,
2001 Colorado Boulevard, Denver, Colorado 80205; www.dmnh.org
and Westcliffe Publishers, Inc., P.O. Box 1261,
Englewood, Colorado 80150; www.westcliffepublishers.com
Printed in Hong Kong through World Print, Ltd.

Cover: Black bear cub/Previous page: Red fox kits

Contents

Canada goose chick

Black bear

Have you ever been hiking and seen a deer? Have you heard an owl hooting at night? Does a woodpecker live in your backyard? Then you know that Colorado is full of critters. More than 900 species, or kinds, of mammals, birds, reptiles, amphibians, and fish live here—on the Eastern Plains, in mountain forests, in the canyons and valleys of western Colorado, even in our cities and towns.

We couldn't include all those species in this book, so we selected the mammals and birds you are most likely to see, or that we hope you will think are the most fun and interesting. You'll meet each animal through a biography that tells about its life. Photos will help you recognize it. We've also included the scientific name that biologists use to identify each animal species. Sometimes these names are a mouthful (the elk's scientific name is *Cervus elaphus!*), but these names help us avoid confusing one animal for another.

Check "Just the Facts" for a description of each animal, what it eats, what kind of habitat it lives in, and where in Colorado you might see it. Watch for

Critters

"On the Trail" tidbits scattered throughout the book. They provide all kinds of fun, handy facts about Colorado critters. You can look up the definitions of words you don't know in the Glossary at the back of the book.

In *On the Trail of Colorado Critters*, you'll meet some of Colorado's best-known mammals and birds. A mammal is a warm-blooded animal that has hair. Mammal mothers give birth to live young, and they make milk to feed their babies. A bird is a warm-blooded animal with feathers. Birds are hatched from eggs laid by the mother.

This book groups mammals or birds together by their physical appearance or lifestyle. To find an animal, think about what it looks like or how it lives. Does it have hoofs and horns? Does it swoop down from the sky to catch its prey? Does it live near water? The chapter titles will give you clues. As you use the book, you will learn more about each animal, how it relates to other species, and where it fits in Colorado's outdoors.

You'll also discover the many adaptations Colorado critters use to make a living. You might think of each species as a handyman with the right tools to get its particular job done. The bobcat has sharp teeth and claws for hunting. The heron has long legs for wading. Adaptations also help animals survive. The skunk uses its "perfume" to keep predators away, and the porcupine is too prickly to touch. Get the point?

Where Critters Live in Colorado

Have you ever climbed a mountain in Colorado? Have you visited the prairie? Then you know our state stretches from low to high. That's from 3,350 feet (1,021 m) at the Kansas border to 14,433 feet (4,399 m) atop Mount Elbert, to be exact! Have you noticed how the trees and the land change as you drive across the state? The changes in elevation give Colorado eight different ecosystems, or zones of plants and animals that are interrelated.

Within these ecosystems are many habitats for wildlife. Habitats provide the food, water, shelter, and space animals need to live. A ponderosa pine forest provides habitat for certain animals. So does a cottonwood grove along a stream. Some animals, such as the coyote, can live in many habitats. Others, such as the pika, depend on just one habitat.

Colorado Ecosystems

Alpine tundra: Treeless land at the tops of mountains with low-growing plants and rocky slopes.

Subalpine forest: Moist, high-elevation forest with subalpine firs and Engelmann spruce.

Montane forest: Low-elevation mountain forest with ponderosa pines on hot, dry, south-facing slopes and Douglas firs on moist, cool, north-facing slopes.

Montane shrubland: Foothills region with shrubs such as Gambel oak and mountain-mahogany.

Piñon-juniper woodland: Dry country found across southern Colorado, with stands of piñon pines and junipers.

Semidesert shrubland: Dry, rough country of western Colorado, dominated by shrubs such as big sagebrush.

Riparian: Moist area along streams, rivers, and ponds, where water-loving plants, such as cottonwood trees and willows, grow.

Grassland: Grassy prairie of eastern Colorado, where few trees grow.

Bald eagles

Critter-Watchers' Code of Conduct

Going outdoors to see animals is like going into someone else's home. Remember to respect the animals. Never shout, throw rocks, or chase them. It's okay to look at their nests and burrows, but then leave them as you found them. Pick up your trash and carry it out. Keep your pets on a leash so they don't chase the animals, or, better yet, leave your pets at home. If you find a baby bird or mammal, leave it alone. It has not been abandoned. Its mother is probably nearby waiting for you to leave.

Respect other people, too. Never go onto private land without permission. If you see someone else watching animals, keep quiet and don't rush up to see what they're looking at. Be careful not to cross in front of them and block their view. Instead, quietly ask them what they see. With everyone looking, you'll see more animals!

Tips for Better Critter Watching

If you were a critter in the forest, and someone came running down the trail, shouting and waving, what would you do? You would run away and hide! Remember that animals are shy. A good way to see them is to find a quiet spot and sit down and wait. If you sit still, you become part of the landscape, and you'll see amazing things. When you're quiet, the animals come out of hiding. They sing their songs, play with their babies, flash their feathers, and flirt with each other. And you would have missed it all if you had been talking or running!

You can still see animals when you're hiking if you move quietly. When you spot a critter, don't move directly at it. The animal will think you are hunting it, and it will run away. Instead, stop and watch. Listen for clues to its location and identity. To get a closer look, start moving slowly, but not straight at the animal. Move in a direction that will take you past it, peeking over to get a good look as you drift by.

If you're really serious about watching wildlife, get a pair of binoculars. You will be amazed at how much more you can see. What you wear in the outdoors matters, too. You will blend into the surroundings better if you wear nature colors, like forest green, brown, and tan. Remember to bring a hat, water bottle, sunscreen, rain gear, and layers of clothing.

Are you ready? Then let's get on the trail of those Colorado critters!

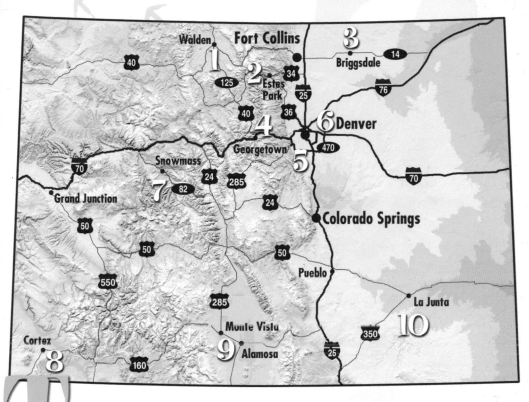

Ten Great Places to See Colorado Critters

A ll of these critter-watching places are on public land. Some have entry fees. Call for more information.

1. Arapaho National Wildlife Refuge (970-723-8202)
2. Rocky Mountain National Park
   (970-586-1206; 970-586-1333 for recorded message)
3. Pawnee National Grassland (970-353-5004)
4. Georgetown State Wildlife Area (303-569-2888)
5. Chatfield State Park (303-791-7275)
6. Rocky Mountain Arsenal National Wildlife Refuge
   (303-289-0400; 303-289-0232)
7. Maroon Lake and Maroon Bells-Snowmass
   Wilderness Area (970-925-3445)
8. Mesa Verde National Park (970-529-4465)
9. Alamosa and Monte Vista National Wildlife Refuges
   (719-589-4021, ext. 101)
10. Picket Wire Canyonlands (719-384-2181)

Hunters with

Does your dog eat broccoli? Does your cat gobble down stewed prunes? Of course not! That's because dogs and cats are carnivores. They eat meat. Wild cousins of dogs and cats, such as coyotes and mountain lions, hunt other animals for food. They are predators, and meat is very important in their diet. Their sharp teeth and claws are designed as tools for catching and killing their food. Large eyes, sharp vision, and good hearing also help these animals hunt and catch their prey.

Even though we call them meat-eaters, most of these hunters also eat food that comes from plants. Though bears seem very fierce, much of the food they eat is plant matter, such as berries and nuts. Animals that can eat lots of different foods are called opportunists. They take advantage of whatever opportunity comes their way for a meal.

Red fox

Coyote

Mountain lion

Tooth and Claw

Black bear

Raccoon

Bobcat

Striped skunk

Coyote
Canis latrans

Where do coyotes live? Just about everywhere. What do they eat? Just about anything. Coyotes are amazingly adaptable animals. They can change what they do, where they live, and what they eat, depending on the situation. When settlers came west and built farms, ranches, and cities, coyotes adapted to living around them. When wolves were killed off, coyotes moved into places where wolves had lived. Now these intelligent animals live throughout Colorado, even in suburban parks and open space.

Coyotes often live in extended families of parents, puppies, and older brothers and sisters. In spring, a coyote pair digs a den and gives birth to a litter of puppies. Once the playful puppies are old enough, they go hunting with their parents. You may hear a coyote family howling together in the evening in a group sing. Coyotes howl to announce their territory—as if to say, "This is our turf!"—and to bond with other pack members. Howling tells other coyotes where the howler is and even its emotional state. Coyotes also talk with yips, growls, body postures, and facial expressions.

Have you heard a coyote howl? Did that howl sound sad to you, or funny or lonely or wild? Coyotes affect people differently. Some people are afraid of them. Others think they are magical or mysterious. Native Americans tell many stories of a special being called Coyote. He was a magical animal who could think and talk like a person. Sometimes he lied or stole things, or he was very brave and saved people. Native people recognize in the wily coyote many of the traits they see in people. What does the coyote mean to you?

Just the Facts

Description: Grayish black body; long, plumed tail; pointed ears; yellow eyes; about 28 lbs (13 kg).

Diet: Rodents, rabbits, carrion, fawns, birds, eggs, berries, nuts, fruit, insects, crops.

Habitat: Grasslands, shrub-lands, mountain meadows, alpine tundra, and piñon-juniper woodlands.

Where to watch: Statewide, especially on the Eastern Plains and in open mountain parks.

(Top) Coyotes are sometimes called Song Dogs for their musical howling.
(Bottom left) Big ears help coyotes hear mice rustling in the grass.
(Bottom right) Year-old coyotes that don't have puppies of their own may help their parents raise their younger brothers and sisters.

On the Trail

If you're on the trail and find what looks like the track of a medium-size dog, you may have found a coyote track. Like their dog cousins, coyotes walk up on their toes. Their tracks show four toes and a large pad. Look for the marks left by their claws.

Red Fox

Vulpes vulpes

Red fox, red fox, where do you roam?
Meadows, woodlands, city parks, I call all
of these home.

Red foxes can live in lots of different habitats.
They usually like to be near water, and they need
enough undergrowth, or tall vegetation, to move
around without being seen. They will live close to
people as long as they have places to hide. Do you
think a red fox might live in a park, golf course,
greenbelt, or cemetery in your neighborhood?

In spring and summer, fox life revolves around
the family. The parents move into an existing
burrow or dig a new one. Here the female gives
birth to a litter of four to six kits. (Baby foxes
are called kits, cubs, or pups.) Both the male
and female hunt for the family, bringing
food to the young. Sometimes female foxes
born the year before that do not have
young of their own will help their parents
by bringing food for the kits. Once the
kits are old enough, they play and sun
themselves outside the den. They tussle
together and pounce on bones and feathers
as if these things were live animals. That's how
kits learn to be foxes. By fall the kits can go out
on their own. The parents usually stay together
and raise another family the next spring.

Foxes have long impressed people because they
are so adaptable and intelligent. Reynard the Fox
is a character in French folklore who triumphs
over brute force with his cleverness. In the stories,
Reynard dresses stylishly and is very handsome.
Don't you think that's a good way to depict
the sleek and beautiful red fox?

Just the Facts

Description: Usually orangish
red body; pale undersides; black
legs; pointed ears; thick, bushy
tail that is three-quarters the
length of the body; 7–15 lbs
(3–7 kg).

Diet: Mice, birds, bird eggs,
berries, fruit, fish, carrion, insects.

Habitat: Meadows, farm fields,
pastures, riparian areas, open
woodlands, city and suburban
parks and open space.

Where to watch: Statewide.

(Left) Red foxes adapt well to living near people.
(Above) Big ears, sharp eyes, and a good sense of smell help foxes find their prey.
(Below) Play-fighting helps red fox kits learn how to get along with other foxes.

On the Trail

What color is a red fox? Well, most of them are red. A few are reddish with a dark cross covering their shoulders and the middle of their back. Some are black with silver-tipped fur. They are called silver foxes. So a silver fox is a red fox that's black. You can't always tell a red fox by its color!

Bobcat
Lynx rufus

A cat named Bob? Actually, the bobcat is named for its bobbed, or short, tail. If you ever go hiking, there's a good chance one has seen you as it watched silently from a hiding place. You don't need to be afraid of bobcats. They are shy and would rather avoid you. Bobcats are about twice the size of a domestic cat. Of all the carnivores, members of the cat family are the most dependent on meat. Bobcats have the usual tools of the hunting cat: forward-facing eyes; curving, retractable claws; long, sharp teeth. Bobcats live in most habitats in Colorado, including farms and city suburbs, but they prefer habitats with lots of places to hide and a variety of small prey.

Bobcats live by themselves, except when the female has a litter of spotted kittens. She hunts for and raises the kittens without any help from a male.

Just the Facts

Description: Tan body with dark spots; short, bobbed tail with black tip; long legs; ruff of fur around face; tufts of fur bristling from tips of ears; 11–31 lbs (5–14 kg).

Diet: Mice, ground and tree squirrels, rabbits, birds, fawns.

Habitat: Piñon-juniper woodlands, low-elevation forests, rough foothills and canyons, shrublands, ranch land.

Where to watch: Statewide, though more common from the Front Range foothills west and across southern Colorado.

Mountain Lion
Felis concolor

Did you know mountain lions purr? Just don't expect one to curl up in your lap. Mountain lions are similar to your pet cat in some ways. Both are equipped with sharp, retractable claws that curve out to grab and hold prey, and both have long, sharp teeth. When your cat is about to pounce on something, does it watch and wait? Mountain lions do the same with their prey. They wait until the best possible moment to pounce, increasing the chances of a safe, successful hunt. Mountain lions can't risk hurting themselves. A lion with an injured paw or a broken leg would soon starve to death.

Notice the mountain lion's large, forward-facing eyes. The lion relies on vision to detect its prey. Its eyes allow it to notice quick movements and to judge the distance to its prey. Mountain lions are also fast and powerful. They have to be to bring down full-grown deer, their main food.

Mountain lions are solitary animals, except when the female has kittens. The kittens are born spotted, but the spots disappear in about a year.

(Top left) Can your cat climb trees? The bobcat can.
(Middle left) Bobcat kittens stay with their mother for about ten months. Then they go off to live alone.
(Right) What about this mountain lion's face tells you it is a hunter? Its big, alert ears and forward-facing eyes.

Just the Facts

Description: Large, sleek, muscular body; tan fur; small ears; rounded head; long, heavy tail; 80–229 lbs (36–104 kg).

Diet: Deer, mice, raccoons, beavers, porcupines, ground squirrels, rabbits; sometimes berries, fish, insects.

Habitat: Rough, broken terrain, especially in canyons and foothills, with open woodlands.

Where to watch: Front Range foothills west across the state.

Striped Skunk
Mephitis mephitis

Pee-yew! Nobody wants to tangle with a skunk, right? Once a predator has been sprayed by the stinky oil of a skunk, it won't bother a skunk again. The skunk wears black and white to be sure other animals recognize it. With these colors, the skunk "tells" other animals, "I am a skunk." Predators quickly learn to pay attention to this warning.

Skunks eat just about anything. Their eyesight isn't very good, so they trundle along sniffing for food. They crack open eggs by throwing them back between their legs against a rock. If you're out in the woods or a field at night, you may hear one rustling noisily in the shrubs and grass. Skunks don't need to be quiet or sneaky like most other animals. They rely on their smelly reputation to protect them from predators.

Just the Facts

Description: Black body with broad white stripe down each side of back; long, bushy tail; 4–10 lbs (2–4.5 kg).
Diet: Insects, mice, ground-nesting birds and their eggs, berries, fruit, grains.
Habitat: Farm fields, pastures, riparian areas, mountain meadows, forests with a lot of understory.
Where to watch: Statewide.

(Above) These three baby skunks are signaling, "Watch out! We're about to spray!"

Raccoon
Procyon lotor

Ever wondered why a raccoon has a black mask across its eyes? You wear a mask on Halloween to hide your identity. The raccoon's mask helps it hide, too. Other nighttime predators can't see the raccoon because its black mask helps its face blend into the darkness.

Raccoons have not always been common in Colorado, but they are adaptable animals. As people changed the plants and landscape of Colorado, they created habitat for raccoons. Now raccoons are growing in number and showing up all over the state.

You can tell if a raccoon has been around by the tracks it leaves in mud. Want to know what the tracks look like? Press your hand, with the fingers spread, on a piece of paper and trace around it. Put little dots in front of the fingers to represent claws. Now you have a good idea of what a raccoon's front tracks look like, although your tracks are much bigger.

Just the Facts

Description: Stocky body; short legs; rounded ears; long, bushy tail with black rings; black mask across eyes; gray fur tipped with black; 6.5–20 lbs (3–9 kg).

Diet: Crayfish, fish, insects, larvae, nuts, seeds, berries, crops, garbage, eggs, small mammals, carrion.

Habitat: Near streams, canals, ponds, lakes; farmland; suburban parks and gardens.

Where to watch: Statewide, but most common at lower elevations in eastern and western Colorado.

(Below) A raccoon's black and gray markings look like shadows. They make the raccoon hard to see at night.

On the Trail

You can help save a bear's life by keeping it out of trouble. If a bear smells food or garbage, it will investigate your house or campsite. When you are in bear country, put garbage in the house or a bearproof trash can or hang it from a tree. In Colorado, wildlife officers must kill any bear that damages property or scares people more than once.

Black Bear

Ursus americanus

What color is a black bear? In Colorado, black bears have as many hair colors as the kids in your class. Their coats range from black to dark brown to cinnamon to blond. Bleaching by the sun can lighten the fur of dark-colored bears.

Bears are magical animals. Why? They die in the fall and are reborn in the spring. At least that's what many cultures thought for centuries. How else could they explain animals that slept through the winter without eating? Of course, bears don't really die every fall. They hibernate, going into a deep sleep to save energy. Their heart rate and metabolism slow way down, but their body temperature doesn't drop much. They can wake up and become active quickly if they're disturbed. Hibernating bears may go for six months without eating, drinking, or going to the bathroom. Females even give birth to tiny, hairless babies during their winter rest.

When bears come out of hibernation, they wander around until their digestive system revs up. Bears belong to the carnivore, or meat-eater, group. They will eat any animal they can catch, but plants provide as much as 90 percent of their diet. By late summer they eat frantically, up to twenty-three hours a day, to store up enough fat to last them through the winter. Insects, nuts, and fruits provide food that is easy to get and high in fat and sugar. Think how many bugs, berries, acorns, and roots a bear must eat to weigh 300 pounds (136 kg)!

(Top left) Despite their fierce reputation, black bears mostly eat plants, including wildflowers.
(Bottom left) Both of these bears are black bears, even though one isn't colored black.
(Right) Black bears can climb trees to safety.

Just the Facts

Description: Large, stocky body; fur ranging in color from black to pale blond; rounded ears; short tail; 130–350 lbs (60–160 kg).

Diet: Acorns, pine nuts, berries, roots, flowers, carrion, insects, small mammals, fawns, birds, eggs.

Habitat: Areas with mature stands of oak brush, chokecherry, and other fruit- and nut-producing shrubs, such as piñon-juniper woodlands; mountain meadows and forests; shrublands.

Where to watch: Statewide, spring through fall.

Hunters from

W ant to be a hawk? Fly way up high in the sky. Then drop down and grab your food with your toes. Now, without using your hands, tear your food up and swallow it. Did we mention that your dinner was a wriggling rabbit? If you were a hunter from the sky—a hawk, eagle, falcon, or owl— this is how you'd get your food. These hunting birds are called birds of prey, or raptors. They have very special tools for the job of hunting: excellent eyesight; sharp, curved beaks; strong feet; sharp, curving claws called talons. The smaller raptors catch prey as small as grasshoppers. The larger ones hunt bigger animals. Birds of prey use different techniques to find and catch the animals they eat. Some of them soar high in the sky searching for food. Others dive through the air at high speed, and some hunt silently in the dark of night. Can you find at least one bird in this chapter for each of these ways of hunting?

Peregrine falcons

Turkey vulture

Red-tailed hawk

the Sky

Bald eagle

Great horned owls

Burrowing owls

Golden eagle

Bald Eagle

Haliaeetus leucocephalus

The bald eagle story teaches us a lot about taking care of the environment. Biologists think there were about 75,000 bald eagles at the time of the Revolutionary War, when the eagle was adopted as our national symbol. By 1967, almost 200 years later, there were only 418 nesting pairs left in the continental United States, and the U.S. Fish and Wildlife Service listed the bald eagle as an endangered species. What had happened?

When wetlands were drained for farming, bald eagle habitat was destroyed. In addition, a pesticide called DDT washed off of farmers' crops and ran into lakes and rivers. The DDT built up in the bodies of fish and poisoned the eagles that ate them. The DDT made the eagles' eggshells so thin the eggs would break. The use of DDT was banned in 1972, and biologists have worked hard to protect bald eagles. Now there are about 4,500 breeding pairs of bald eagles outside of Alaska and lots more nonbreeding birds. Hundreds of bald eagles spend their winters in Colorado. Bald eagles are expected to be completely removed from the endangered species list in 2000.

A bald eagle hunts by flying over a lake or river. When it spots a fish in the water, it drops down and grabs the fish with its huge, strong talons—zap! The bald eagle doesn't have feathers on its legs. Feathers would just drag it down in the water. Sometimes bald eagles are pirates. Instead of catching their own prey, they chase a smaller hawk and scare it into dropping its meal. The bald eagle snags a free lunch.

Just the Facts

Description: Very large, dark brown body; white head and tail; yellow beak and legs; 31–37 in. (79–94 cm) from beak to tail; 6–7.5 ft (1.8–2.3 m) wingspan.

Diet: Fish, prairie dogs, carrion, rabbits, water birds.

Habitat: Riparian areas; grasslands and prairie dog towns in winter.

Where to watch: Rivers and reservoirs of eastern Colorado, Colorado River and tributaries, winter; Yampa River, southwestern Colorado, Barr Lake State Park, summer.

(Left) *The bald eagle tears meat into bite-size chunks with its sharp, curved beak.*
(Above) *This raptor uses its grasping talons, not a fishing pole, to catch fish.*
(Below) *These are all bald eagles. From left to right: a mature adult, a young bird that's less than a year old, a 2- or 3-year-old eagle.*

On the Trail

If a bald eagle sat in the middle of your sofa and spread its wings, the tips would stick out over the sofa arms. The bald eagle's huge size will help you identify it when it is flying or perched in a tree. What's the main feature you'll notice? Its gleaming white head. Bald eagles don't get their white heads until they're 4 or 5 years old.

Golden Eagle

Aquila chrysaetos

The bald eagle may be our national symbol, but the golden eagle is the bird of kings. It is found all over the world and has been the symbol of royalty in Europe for centuries. Kings used trained golden eagles to hunt other animals and bring them back to their master. These magnificent hunters can soar on their broad wings for hours. They can also plummet down onto prey like falcons do.

Golden eagles are named for the pale, golden feathers on their heads and necks. They have smaller heads than bald eagles, and feathers cover their legs down to their toes. They have very strong feet with sharp talons. Three toes face forward and one faces back. When an eagle grabs a rabbit, the eagle's feet squeeze its prey's body and the talons dig in. The rabbit's struggles cause the eagle to squeeze tighter until the rabbit dies.

Just the Facts

Description: Very large, dark brown body; golden head and neck; dark bill and talons; 30–40 in. (76–102 cm) from beak to tail; 6.5–7.5 ft (2.0–2.3 m) wingspan.
Diet: Jackrabbits, small mammals, snakes, fawns, birds.
Habitat: Cliffs and canyons near open country, grasslands, shrublands, pine forests.
Where to watch: Statewide, but particularly in northwestern Colorado in summer.

(Below) What's the difference between the golden eagle's head and the bald eagle's?

Summer and Winter Hawks

The **rough-legged hawk** (*Buteo lagopus*) arrives from northern Canada in mid-October and stays until March. These winter hawks are named for the fluffy feathers on their legs. Despite being the same size as red-tailed and Swainson's hawks, rough-legs have small feet. One way to tell them apart from other big hawks is where they perch in a tree. Rough-legs sit on the thin, outer branches because their feet are too small to hold onto big branches.

The **Swainson's hawk** (*Buteo swainsoni*) arrives in April to nest in trees and bluffs on Colorado's Eastern Plains. You will recognize this summer hawk by the coppery brown plumage that covers its head and breast. Despite its large size, this hawk's favorite food is grasshoppers. It will grab a grasshopper with its foot, then eat the insect from its talon while flying. In September, Swainson's hawks gather in big groups to migrate to Argentina's grasslands for the winter.

(Top left) *The rough-legged hawk tells you its identity by perching on slender limbs in treetops.*
(Top right) *You can tell a Swainson's hawk by the copper-colored hood over its head and breast.*

Red-tailed Hawk

Buteo jamaicensis

Ready to scream like a hawk? Shout *Keeer!*, making the sound go down as if you were falling off a cliff. You've heard the scream of a red-tailed hawk many times, although you may not know it. The red-tail's scream is used as a background sound in movies and television shows all the time.

What's the best clue to identify a red-tailed hawk? You guessed it. The bird has a rusty-red tail that is easy to see when it is flying. You can often see it when the bird is perched, too.

In midday, hawks use their big, wide wings to soar on rising columns of warm air called thermals. If you're out watching hawks in early morning when the air is cool, notice how hard the hawks have to flap their wings to gain altitude.

Are you hawkeyed? The hawk's eye is an amazing hunting tool. Each eye has two fovea, or focus points. Your eye only has one. One fovea gives the hawk sharp vision. The other helps it perceive depth very accurately. Could a hawk drop down from the sky onto a rabbit if it had bad depth perception? A hawk's eye also has a million visual cells per millimeter. Your eye has about 200,000. If you were standing on the tenth floor of a building, could you spot a mouse on the ground? A hawk could. It can clearly see a mouse moving in the grass from 100 feet (30 m) up in the sky.

Just the Facts

Description: Large, dark brown body; pale breast; rusty-red tail; some red-tails all dark or very pale with light head and tail; 22 in. (56 cm) from beak to tail; 3.5–4.5 ft (1.2–1.5 m) wingspan.

Diet: Rabbits, mice, other small mammals, snakes, lizards, frogs, birds.

Habitat: Grasslands, farm fields, pastures, wooded areas along waterways, mountain forests.

Where to watch: Statewide, year-round.

(Left) Red-tailed hawks soar high on broad wings.
(Above) Red-tails use their excellent vision to spot their prey.
(Below) This immature red-tailed hawk has brown plumage speckled with white. Its red tail won't develop until its second year.

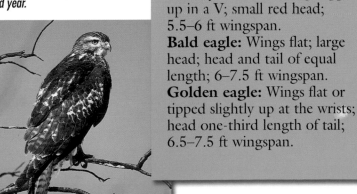

On the Trail

Here are some tips to identifying raptors in flight:

Red-tailed hawk: Wings flat; "bulging," rounded wings; 3.5–4.5 ft wingspan.

Turkey vulture: Wings tipped up in a V; small red head; 5.5–6 ft wingspan.

Bald eagle: Wings flat; large head; head and tail of equal length; 6–7.5 ft wingspan.

Golden eagle: Wings flat or tipped slightly up at the wrists; head one-third length of tail; 6.5–7.5 ft wingspan.

Peregrine Falcon
Falco peregrinus

Would you want to hunt like the peregrine falcon does? First, find yourself a canyon. Then fly up to a high cliff. When you spot a swallow flying below, point your head downward and jump into the air. Flap a few times, then fold your wings. Don't worry if you get up to 200 miles per hour (320 kph). You're a falcon. As you reach the swallow, pull up and strike it with your closed talons, like fists. As the bird falls, dive on it again, and grab the swallow from the sky with your feet.

Peregrine falcons almost disappeared from most of the lower forty-eight states because of DDT poisoning. By the 1970s, only four pairs of peregrines nested in Colorado. Through the 1980s, Colorado biologists hatched 500 young peregrines in captivity and then carefully placed them in wild nests. Now there are more than ninety active nests in Colorado. In 1999, the peregrine falcon was taken off the endangered species list.

Just the Facts

Description: Slate blue back and wings; pale undersides with dark barring; slate blue "helmet" and "sideburns"; long tail; pointed, tapering wings; 16–21 in. (41–53 cm) from beak to tail; 3–4 ft (0.9–1.2 m) wingspan.

Diet: Songbirds, ducks, some insects.

Habitat: Cliffs, canyons, rocky habitats, urban areas with tall buildings, reservoirs during migration and in winter.

Where to watch: Western Colorado, Flatirons near Boulder, Roxborough State Park in summer; statewide during migration.

American Kestrel
Falco sparverius

Take the fierceness of an eagle. Add sharp talons and beak and the eyes of a hawk. Mix in swiftness on the wing. Roll it all up in a package a little bigger than a robin. Paint it reddish brown and steel blue. Presto, you have made a kestrel, America's smallest falcon. You may have passed by a kestrel a hundred times without realizing that the bird perched on a wire above you was a bird of prey. Kestrels are proof you don't have to be big to be a fierce hunter.

Kestrels will catch mice and other small animals, but their favorite food is grasshoppers. You may see a kestrel hovering over a grassy field like a helicopter. It has seen something moving below and is waiting to pounce.

In spring, male kestrels fly patterns in the air to impress females. Listen for their *Killy, killy, killy* calls.

Both the peregrine falcon **(left)** and the American kestrel **(right)** are swift-flying falcons. Notice how small their beaks are compared to eagles' beaks? Falcons eat smaller prey than eagles do. **(Far left)** Peregrine falcons nest on remote cliff ledges, called aeries.

Just the Facts

Description: Two stripes down each cheek; 10.5 in. (26.5 cm) from beak to tail; 2 ft (0.6 m) wingspan. Male: rusty-red back and tail; peach breast; steel blue wings and cap. Female: reddish brown body; blue cap; pale underparts; slightly larger than male.

Diet: Grasshoppers, other insects, mice, lizards, snakes, frogs, birds.

Habitat: Grasslands, farms and ranches, mountain parks and meadows, shrublands.

Where to watch: Statewide, but most abundant on the Eastern Plains.

Turkey Vulture
Cathartes aura

Which animal has the grossest job in nature? The turkey vulture. It eats dead stuff. It sticks its head into the carcasses of dead animals. Its bare red head has no feathers so it's easier to keep clean, considering where that head goes. The turkey vulture does an important job, though. It helps clean up animal remains and recycle them. You might think of the vulture as nature's garbage disposal.

Turkey vultures can stay aloft for hours without flapping their wings. They can spot an animal carcass on the ground from two-and-a-half miles (4 km) up. At that distance, you couldn't even see the vulture as a speck in the sky! Some Native Americans thought the high-soaring vultures communicated with the gods and carried the souls of the dead to heaven.

The turkey vulture is one of the few birds with a good sense of smell. Maybe to a vulture, a dead skunk smells as good as chocolate chip cookies baking in the oven smell to us.

Just the Facts

Description: Black body; bare red head; broad, wide wings, spanning 5.5–6 ft (1.7–1.8 m); 27 in. (69 cm) from beak to tail.
Diet: Carrion.
Habitat: Grasslands, shrublands, farm fields and open country, rocky terrain and cliffs near open country.
Where to watch: Eastern and western foothills and western valleys, summer; Eastern Plains, spring and fall.

(Top left) In fall, migrating turkey vultures gather in huge, soaring flocks.
(Top right) A turkey vulture's head has no feathers. What we see is its red skin.

Burrowing Owl

Athene cunicularia

Ever seen a prairie dog fly? That's what some people think is happening when they see a burrowing owl flying through a prairie dog town. These little ground owls are about the same shape and height as a prairie dog. In spring, they lay their eggs in abandoned prairie dog burrows. By June, the baby owls sit on top of the burrows, waiting for their parents to bring them food. By late September they are fully grown and ready to fly south for the winter.

If you could slither down into their burrow, you might be scared by a rattling sound, like a rattlesnake. It's just a sound the baby owls make for protection. If a predator thinks a rattlesnake is in the burrow, it will leave the owls alone.

The destruction of many prairie dog towns has hurt burrowing owls, and their numbers have gone way down. Now the burrowing owl is a threatened species in Colorado, meaning it needs protection to avoid becoming an endangered species.

Just the Facts

Description: Small brown body streaked and flecked with white; long legs; yellow eyes; white eyebrows; 9.5 in. (24 cm) from beak to tail; 22 in. (56 cm) wingspan.

Diet: Grasshoppers, mice, snakes, toads, lizards.

Habitat: Prairie dog towns and nearby open land.

Where to watch: Eastern Colorado, from the Front Range to Kansas; around Grand Junction.

(Below) In early summer, young owls cluster together on top of their burrow.

Great Horned Owl
Bubo virginianus

Take your fingers and put them in your ears. Now move your left finger down an inch. Move your right finger up an inch. If you were a great horned owl, this is where your ears would be. The owl's ears, which are hidden by feathers, are lopsided for a reason. They help the owl locate prey. Try moving your head around. Notice how you hear sounds differently in each ear? By tilting and moving its head, the owl locates a squeaking mouse hidden in the grass. When the sound to each ear is equal, the owl's vision is on a straight line with the mouse. Then whammo! The owl snares the mouse in its talons. The owl's hearing is so good that it can find prey in complete darkness.

Look at the owl's face. Compare it to one of the songbirds in "Winging from Prairie to Peak." Then look at your own face in the mirror. Which bird do you look most like? Both you and the owl have large, forward-facing eyes. You both depend a lot on sight. The owl's eyes are about the same size as yours but a hundred times sharper. Even on a moonless night, this nocturnal hunter can see a mouse in the grass where we would see nothing but black.

Great horned owls are such fierce hunters they are called winged tigers. They eat all kinds of small animals. They are one of the few predators that will catch skunks. Although they have great hearing and vision, owls have practically no sense of smell. To them, the skunk is just a slow-moving meal.

Just the Facts

Description: Large, brown body; black barring on feathers; big yellow eyes; two feathery "horns" on head; gold feathery disks framing face; 22 in. (56 cm) from beak to tail; 3–5 ft (0.9–1.5 m) wingspan.
Diet: Rabbits, mice, skunks, birds, snakes, toads.
Habitat: Woodlands near water and open country; suburban and urban parks and open space; pine forests.
Where to watch: Statewide.

(Left) The "horns" on top of a great horned owl's head aren't ears or horns. They are just tufts of feathers.
(Below) A young owlet finishes a mouse meal. One owl may kill 2,000 mice a year.

On the Trail

You can become a skilled wildlife spotter by training yourself to look for shapes that seem out of place. To spot great horned owls in winter, look for large, dark, cylindrical shapes sitting on tree limbs near the trunk, not out at the edge.

Hoofs and

Imagine if, instead of feet and toes, you had hard, shiny black hoofs to stand on. And what if you had to carry a pair of horns or antlers on your head? Lots of animals in Colorado are made that way. In this chapter you'll meet seven large Colorado mammals that come with hoofs and headgear.

These animals move across prairies and mountain meadows, through forests and along streams, grazing on grass or nibbling on twigs and leaves. Some have antlers. Others have horns. They don't use their headgear to get food. Instead, their horns and antlers help them relate to each other. Males use their headgear to challenge other males during the breeding season. Some fight each other with their antlers or horns. Large antlers or horns tell females that a male is strong and healthy and would make a good father.

Animals with hoofs are actually walking on their very thick, hard toenails. If you could run on your toenails, your leg would extend further, and you could push off more with each step. Hoofs are an adaptation that helps these animals run faster, giving them the speed they need to outrun predators.

Bighorn sheep

White-tailed deer

Headgear

Moose

Mountain goats

Pronghorn

Elk

Mule deer

On the Trail

Each spring, male members of the deer family grow a new pair of antlers. The antlers are covered with velvet—soft, fuzzy tissue that nurtures the growing antlers. In summer, the antlers harden to feel like bone, and the deer rubs his antlers against trees to scrape off the dried-up velvet. By fall his antlers are hard and polished. In late winter, the antlers fall off, and the cycle starts again.

White-tailed Deer
Odocoileus virginianus

Have you ever seen a flash of white in the trees by a prairie stream? Did it bob away through the trees? What you saw was the tail of a white-tailed deer. When white-tailed deer are frightened, they flick up their tails. The white hair on the underside of the tail makes a sudden flash. The flash warns other deer that danger is near. All the deer bound away with their white tails flying like flags. The tails also signal predators, as if to say, "We see you!"

White-tails are shy and easily frightened. They hide among trees and shrubs along rivers. When settlers in eastern Colorado planted trees, they created habitat for white-tails. The deer migrated here along newly wooded waterways. Now white-tails are common in eastern Colorado.

In spring, female deer, called does, give birth to one to three tiny, spotted fawns. The fawns can stand and walk soon after birth. They lose their spots when they are 3 or 4 months old.

If you look closely, you can tell if a deer antler came from a white-tailed deer or a mule deer. A white-tail's antler has one main beam, or branch. The tines, or projections, stick up from this main beam. People judge the age and size of a male deer, called a buck, by the number of tines on each antler. That's what it means if you hear someone mention a "five-point buck." Find out about the mule deer's antlers on page 41.

(Top left) A spotted fawn lies hidden in tall grass. Its mother will come back once danger passes.
(Left) You'd be lucky to see a white-tail buck like this one. These deer are very shy animals.
(Right) White-tails toss up their tails like flags when danger threatens.

Just the Facts

Description: Reddish brown body (brownish gray in winter); wide, flat, bushy tail brown on top and white underneath; 39 in. (99 cm) tall at shoulder; 90–300 lbs (40–136 kg). Male: antlers.

Diet: Tender shoots, buds, leaves, and twigs of trees and shrubs; flowering plants; some grass; some crops.

Habitat: Woodlands along prairie streams; farm fields and orchards near rivers.

Where to watch: Eastern Colorado, especially along the South Platte, Arkansas, and Republican Rivers.

39

On the Trail

Colorado has a large population of mule deer. You can often see them in fields and grazing pastures in eastern Colorado. Mule deer do the best in broken terrain (land with lots of gullies) where shrubs grow, such as in western Colorado. Why would shrublands with lots of gullies be good places for them to live?

Mule Deer
Odocoileus hemionus

Why do you suppose this deer is called a mule? Do you think it's stubborn? Does it have a loud, braying voice? Look closely at the photos. This deer has very long ears, like a mule. Sometimes you may see mule deer lying down in tall grass. Their long ears give them away. The ears stick up like a V. That way, the hidden animal can still listen for danger, with its big ears gathering sound like a radar dish.

November and December are the mating season for deer. During this time, the necks of deer bucks (male deer) swell up. They almost look like pro wrestlers! Bucks become short-tempered and might shadowbox at shrubs with their antlers. Shadowboxing is practice for fighting antler-to-antler with other bucks.

Except during mating season, bucks often hang out with one or more other males. After the fawns are born, does gather in small groups with other does, fawns, and yearlings (deer that are a year old).

You can easily tell if a deer antler came from a mule deer. The mule deer's antler forks into two beams, or branches. Each of these branches then forks into two or more projections, called tines. As a deer grows older, it gets bigger antlers with more tines. Old bucks can have six or more tines,

called points, on each antler. Read about the white-tailed deer's antlers on page 39. Remember, only male deer grow antlers.

Just the Facts

Description: Large, brown body; whitish throat; white rump; long, slender tail with black tip; black band across forehead; very large ears; 28–42 in. (71–107 cm) tall at shoulder; 155 lbs (70 kg) on average. Male: antlers.
Diet: Tender buds, shoots, leaves,and twigs of shrubs and trees; flowering plants, some grass.
Habitat: Eastern grasslands, farm fields, grazing pastures, mountain woodlands and meadows, western shrublands.
Where to watch: Statewide.

(Top left) Tiny blood vessels make up the velvet that nurtures the growing antlers of these mule deer bucks.
(Bottom left) During the fall mating season, a buck's neck swells up, making him look bigger.
(Left) This doe's twin fawns are not unusual. Sometimes mule deer have triplets.

On the Trail

Early morning or evening are the best times to see elk. This is when they come out of the forest into open meadows to feed. It is best to watch from inside your car. Elk won't be as worried by a car as by the shape of a human. Never approach elk closely. They might charge at you.

(Above) You wouldn't want to get this close to a young male elk on your own. Use binoculars or a telephoto lens.
(Below) A herd of elk grazes undisturbed in a high mountain meadow in Rocky Mountain National Park.
(Right) A bull elk bugles to attract a mate.

Elk
Cervus elaphus

Visit a mountain meadow on an evening in early October, and you may hear some very spooky screams. Don't worry. No one's in trouble. That sound is the bugling of bull elk, which means it's autumn in the high country.

Bull, or male, elk bugle during the fall mating season, called the rut. They bellow to challenge other males and to attract females, called cow elk. Maybe they also bugle just to let off a little steam. Starting low and hollow, the call rises to a shrill, whistling screech. It tapers off into a series of *chuffs* and *whuffs*. Imagine if you lived in a big open meadow. A high-pitched bugle would be a good way to shout across at another elk. Bugling is kind of the elk version of "king of the mountain." You may even see two bull elk fight antler-to-antler.

Most of the year elk live in two separate social groups. The bulls gather into bachelor herds. The cow elk and their calves live together in another herd. Elk spend summer in high mountain meadows. As winter approaches, they migrate to lower elevations. Why would they migrate for the winter?

At one time, elk lived all across Colorado, even on the Eastern Plains. Then about 150 years ago, lots of miners and settlers started coming to Colorado. Many elk were shot to be sold for food. By the early 1900s, only about 500 to 1,000 elk still survived here. The laws were changed to protect elk. More elk were brought in from Yellowstone National Park and released in the mountains. Today more than 200,000 elk live in Colorado. How many elk have you seen?

Just the Facts

Description: Large, pale brown body; chocolate brown head, neck, and legs; creamy white rump. Male: large antlers with many tines; up to 5 ft (1.5 m) tall at shoulder; up to 1,000 lbs (454 kg). Female: smaller than male; no antlers.

Diet: Grass, flowering plants, tender new growth of shrubs and trees.

Habitat: Forests and meadows of mountains, foothills, and canyons; alpine tundra.

Where to watch: Eastern Slope foothills west across state.

Moose
Alces alces

Spread the fingers of both hands. Now touch the tips of your thumbs to each side of your head. You have a pair of moose antlers! Only male moose grow antlers, which can weigh as much as fifty-five pounds (25 kg). Imagine carrying that weight around on your head! Like other members of the deer family, moose lose their antlers each winter. They grow new ones in time for the fall mating season.

Moose like to hang out in wetlands. They have long legs so they can wade into marshes and flooded meadows. They eat aquatic plants and buds of shrubs and trees that grow along streams.

Moose did not used to be common in Colorado. To establish a population of moose here, the Colorado Division of Wildlife released moose in North Park in 1978. Later they released them in the mountains of southern Colorado. Now Colorado's moose are well established and going strong.

Just the Facts

Description: Very large, dark brown body; big, rounded nose. Male: up to 7 ft (2.1 m) tall at shoulder; up to 1,000 lbs (454 kg); large antlers with flat, wide branches. Female: smaller than male; no antlers.

Diet: Stems, leaves, buds, and bark of shrubs and trees that grow along streams; aquatic plants.

Habitat: Wet meadows, marshes, along streams.

Where to watch: North Park, eastern San Juan Mountains along Rio Grande River.

(Above) Mountain wetlands are a key habitat for moose.

Pronghorn
Antilocapra americana

Can an animal run as fast as a car? The next time you're on the interstate, ask the driver to go sixty miles per hour (96 kph). That's how fast a pronghorn can run. If you tried to sneak up on one, it would race off before you got close. Its big eyes act like telescopes, so it can see you when you're still far away. As it was running off, you would see a flash of white. When a pronghorn is startled, its white rump hairs stand up as a warning signal to other pronghorn.

The pronghorn is named for its horns, which fork at the end. One of the tips curves over, like a prong. Make a fist, then spread your thumb and first finger as far apart as you can. That's what the tip of the pronghorn's horn looks like. Each fall, after the mating season, the horns fall off, like the antlers of a deer. Then the pronghorn grows new horns. The horns are made of a material like our hair. Both males and females grow horns.

(Far right) *The pronghorn is one of the fastest animals on earth. It lives in wide open spaces where there is lots of running room.*
(Right) *A pronghorn buck can detect movement from a mile or more away.*

Just the Facts

Description: Reddish brown body; white undersides and rump; two white bands on throat; black chin-strap on adult males; large, triangular head; large eyes; dark horns; about 3 ft (0.9 m) tall at shoulder; 80–150 lbs (36–68 kg).
Diet: Shrubs, such as bitterbrush and sagebrush; flowering plants; very little grass.
Habitat: Open grasslands, prairies, mountain parks, shrublands.
Where to watch: Eastern Colorado and open mountain parks and valleys across the state.

Mountain Goat

Oreamnos americanus

If you climb up on top of a Colorado mountain, you just might meet a nanny with her kid. They'll both have long white hair, and she'll have curving black horns. How is this possible? They're mountain goats, not people. A female mountain goat is called a nanny, and a baby goat is called a kid. Male mountain goats are called billies.

Mountain goats didn't used to live in Colorado. Starting in the 1940s, the Colorado Division of Wildlife brought mountain goats here from other western states and released them. Now groups of mountain goats live on a few specific mountains and mountain ranges. If you're hiking on a mountaintop in these areas, keep your eyes peeled for tufts of white mountain goat hair snagged on bushes and rocks.

The higher mountain goats can live on a mountain, the better they seem to like it. They seldom move down below timberline. That's why their thick, warm coat is so important. It helps them survive the severe winter weather. Goats often bound around on steep, rocky slopes. You would think they would fall, but they don't. Mountain goats have "suction cups" on their hoofs—soft, spongy bottoms that help the goats cling to the rocks.

In spring and summer, billies live together in bachelor herds. Nannies live in herds with their kids and older young, called yearlings. In the fall, during the mating season, the billies begin joining the herds of nannies and kids. If one billy meets another, he may act fierce and try to scare off the other male by waving his horns, but two billies rarely fight. Kids are born in the spring.

Just the Facts

Description: Dense, long, white or cream-colored hair on body; long face with hairy beard; hoofs, eyes, nose, and slender curving horns all shiny black; 3–3.5 ft (0.9–1.1 m) tall at shoulder; 90–300 lbs (40–136 kg). Female: smaller than male; smaller horns.

Diet: Grass; flowering plants; tender buds, shoots, and leaves of shrubs.

Habitat: Rocky slopes and alpine tundra, ridgetops, open areas at timberline.

Where to watch: Mount Evans, Gore Range, Collegiate Peaks, San Juan Mountains.

On the Trail

Do you know the difference between antlers and horns? Antlers are shed each year. Horns are permanent. Male deer, elk, and moose grow antlers. Both male and female mountain goats and bighorn sheep have horns, like cattle do. Antlers are made of bony material. Horns are made from stuff similar to our finger-nails. Check page 45 to see where pronghorn fit in.

(Left) This steep ice wall doesn't stop a sharp-hoofed mountain goat.
(Above) A heavy, woolly coat keeps the mountain goat warm.
(Below) A nanny with her kid.

Bighorn Sheep

Ovis canadensis

If you want to see a real nature show, watch the Battle of the Bighorn Rams in November and December. You won't find this spectacular contest on cable TV. You'll have to head for open valleys in the mountains, where bighorn sheep gather during the winter breeding season.

Male sheep, called rams, compete to get the attention of female sheep. Running straight at each other, two rams lower their heads and crash head-on, butting their horns with great force. Sometimes the crash can be heard a mile away. After clashing, each ram holds his head up and turns it side-to-side, displaying his horns. Two rams may butt heads over and over. Finally one backs off, and the other is the winner.

If you rammed your head with a friend, it would hurt! How do you suppose the rams do it without getting a terrible headache? Above the forehead, their skulls are spongy inside. That spongy structure absorbs the force from bashing heads. It's like jumping onto a firm mattress instead of a hard floor.

Female sheep are called ewes (pronounced YOOZ). Except during the breeding season, they live in herds with other ewes and their lambs. The rams gather in small bachelor herds with other rams.

For many people, bighorn sheep represent the wildness of Colorado's mountains. At one time, bighorns lived across much more of our state. Now they live only in remote mountain areas. Human activity has pushed them out of other places, although sometimes they get used to the noise and movement of people. Have you ever seen them grazing next to Interstate 70 by the town of Georgetown, as noisy cars and trucks race past?

Just the Facts

Description: Pale gray body; 110–280 lbs (50–127 kg). Male: heavy horns that curl around face. Female: short, slender horns that curve back slightly.

Diet: Grasses; tender leaves, buds, and twigs of shrubs and trees, especially willows.

Habitat: Steep, rocky, grassy mountain slopes.

Where to watch: High mountain areas through the central and western part of the state; Mount Evans, Rocky Mountain National Park, Georgetown State Wildlife Area.

(Top) Scent is an important source of information for bighorn sheep.
(Middle left) Ewes with their lambs stand alert and watchful.
(Middle right) Rocky Mountain National Park is one good place to see our official state animal.
(Bottom) During mating season, bighorn rams fight by butting heads. Their skulls, with horns, can weigh more than 38 pounds (17 kg).

Chiselers

An entire world of critters bustles and chews around us. They are the chiselers, the gnawing animals. They live in trees, on the ground, underground, and even in the water. Can you find an animal from each of these habitats in this chapter?

Teeth are extremely important to the chiselers. Their front teeth are long and sharp and grow differently from yours. Your teeth grew in and stopped. A chiseler's front teeth never stop growing. Chiselers chew so much that their teeth wear away. Ever-growing teeth help them keep on chiseling. If a chiseler ever stopped chewing, its teeth would grow and grow, and it would be in big trouble. So a chiseler chews to live, and lives to chew!

Chiselers are mainly plant-eaters, and they include rabbits and rodents. Squirrels, beavers, porcupines, and prairie dogs are examples of rodents. How are rabbits different from rodents? If you could look in a rabbit's mouth, you would find that instead of just two top front teeth, it has four—two in front, and two right behind them. Rabbits and their relatives also have short tails, or none at all.

Cottontail

Pika

Yellow-bellied marmot

Black-tailed prairie dog

Fox squirrel

Abert's squirrel

Black-tailed jackrabbit

American beaver

Golden-mantled ground squirrel

On the Trail

Have you ever walked through a prairie dog town? Did you activate the prairie dogs' warning system? When prairie dog sentries notice something scary, they start barking loudly, *Yip, yip, yip!* That translates as "Danger! Dive for cover!" Scientists have found that prairie dogs use different barks, depending on whether the danger is a four-legged creature or a threat from the sky.

(Above) *This young prairie dog identifies an adult by sniffing it.*
(Left) *Tossing its head back and barking as it jumps up on its hind legs, this prairie dog performs a "jump-yip" display.*
(Right) *Eyes set at the top of their heads help prairie dogs spot predators.*

Black-tailed Prairie Dog
Cynomys ludovicianus

What animals live in a town? Black-tailed prairie dogs, of course. Prairie dogs are actually ground squirrels. Each prairie dog family lives in a burrow, and they have lots of neighbors. All those burrows together form a prairie dog town. Do you play with the kids next door? Do your parents visit outside with your friends' parents? You live in a community with other people. A prairie dog town is the animal version of your community.

If you could slither down a prairie dog burrow, you would find some rooms for sleeping, some rooms for storing food, and even a bathroom! You would also find a back door. If a predator comes in one entrance after them, the prairie dog family can escape out another hole.

When you pass a prairie dog town, all those animals scurrying around probably make you think there must be billions of prairie dogs out there. Actually, there are only about 2 percent of the prairie dogs around that used to be here. That's how much prairie dog populations have shrunk since settlers came west. Prairie dog towns once covered much of eastern Colorado. Prairie dogs, however, ate grass that ranchers needed for their cows. The rodents also lived where farmers wanted to plant crops, so people killed lots of prairie dogs. Now, as cities along the Front Range grow, prairie dogs are being killed to make room for houses and businesses. What will hawks, owls, and coyotes eat if all the prairie dogs are gone?

Just the Facts

Description: Plump, tan body; short legs; round head; medium-length, black-tipped tail; 12–16 in. (30–41 cm), including tail; 1–3 lbs (0.5–1.4 kg).

Diet: Grass, flowering plants, shrubs, seeds.

Habitat: Grasslands, pastures, vacant lots, undeveloped land.

Where to watch: Open land of eastern Colorado west to the foothills.

Golden-mantled Ground Squirrel

Spermophilus lateralis

Have you ever been on a picnic in the mountains and had an animal that looked like a big chipmunk show up looking for food? That was a golden-mantled ground squirrel. It looks a little like its cousin, the chipmunk, but its color is faded, like it went through a washing machine too many times.

During the cold mountain winters, ground squirrels hibernate in their dens. What energy their body does use comes from stored body fat. Biologists aren't sure what triggers a ground squirrel to wake up in spring. Hibernating animals might have an internal clock that wakes them up. Factors like the ground getting warmer may also help.

By the way, did you give that ground squirrel any picnic snacks? It's not a good idea. Feeding human food to wild animals teaches them not to fear people, and it's probably not healthy for them. They get the nutrition they need from wild foods.

Just the Facts

Description: Medium-size, light brown body; red-brown "mantle" over head and shoulders; no stripes on head; dark stripe next to white one down each side of back; tail hairy but not bushy; 9.5–12 in. (24–30 cm), including 3–4.5 in. (7–12 cm) tail; 6–10 oz (170–283 g).

Diet: Seeds, wildflowers, green plants, fungi.

Habitat: Rocky slopes in open mountain woodlands.

Where to watch: Mountains and mesas of central and western Colorado.

Chipmunks

One Colorado animal you are sure to see if you visit the mountains is a chipmunk. Maybe you'll see one stuffing its cheeks full of food to carry back to its den. Chipmunks live in open, sunny areas near rock piles they can run into for safety.

The **Colorado chipmunk** *(Tamias quadrivittatus)* lives in southern Colorado and the central mountains. It has a black stripe down its back flanked by white and reddish-brown stripes.

The **least chipmunk** *(Tamias minimus)* lives across the state from the Front Range mountains west. It has five black stripes down its back, with white stripes between them, and distinct black-and-white stripes across its eyes. You can also identify the least chipmunk by its smaller size and its behavior. It darts around nervously, in quick little spurts of activity.

(Top left) To distinguish it from a chipmunk, look for the golden-mantled ground squirrel's paler fur and stripeless head.
(Top right) Cheeks make handy carrying pouches.
(Below) Bright white eye stripes, a long tail, and nervous behavior help identify the least chipmunk.

On the Trail

Ready to become a wildlife detective? Sometimes you have to look for clues to tell apart species that look alike. Next time a little brown animal with dark stripes on its back crosses your path, ask yourself, "Is it a chipmunk or a ground squirrel?" Practice your observation skills. How big is it? What color or patterns do you see? How is it behaving? Then compare your notes to the information in this guide to solve the case.

Pine Squirrel
Tamiasciurus hudsonicus

Have you ever hiked in a mountain forest and been scolded by a fluffy-tailed little pine squirrel? You heard the squirrel version of "Get out of my room!" Pine squirrels, or chickarees, are very territorial. They don't like anyone else coming into the place where they live. Pretend you are a pine squirrel. A stranger is walking through your patch of forest. Time to tell him off! Press your tongue to the top of your mouth, right behind your teeth. Now, make a clicking sound— *Tsik, tsik, tsik.* You can now speak "pine squirrel."

In late summer, pinecones rain down onto the forest floor. The pine squirrels are busily cutting the cones to store for winter food. One squirrel can cut down a cone every two or three seconds. Think how many cones it could gather in the time it takes you to make a sandwich.

Just the Facts

Description: Small gray body, lighter undersides, dark stripes on sides; long furry tail; 12–14 in. (30–35 cm), including 4.5–5.5 in. (11.5–13.5 cm) tail; 6.5–9 oz (190–260 g).

Diet: Seeds of conifers; mushrooms and other fungi; buds, berries, and leaves of plants.

Habitat: Coniferous forests.

Where to watch: Foothills and mountains of central and western Colorado.

(Above) Scientists estimate that one pine squirrel can store 16,000 pinecones per year.

Fox Squirrel

Sciurus niger

What animal lives in your backyard, can hang upside down by its toenails, and "talks" by waving its tail? If you said a fox squirrel, you're right.

As you might guess, trees are very important to fox squirrels. They run up trees for safety, using their sharp claws to climb the bark. Have you ever seen a big clump of leaves and sticks high in a tree? That is a squirrel's nest, where the squirrel raises its babies and stays warm in winter. Fox squirrels don't hibernate but store food to live on during the winter months.

Squirrels use their tails to communicate. They can challenge each other with their tail-waving or indicate that they are excited or friendly. If a squirrel suspects a predator is hiding nearby, it flicks its tail to make the predator show itself. Squirrels also communicate by chattering. Can you understand what the squirrels in your yard are saying?

(Below) The fox squirrel's scientific name means "shade-tail," for its bushy tail that can shade its head like an umbrella.

Just the Facts

Description: Reddish brown or gray-brown coat; long, bushy tail; small ears; large eyes; flexible paws; 17.5–23.5 in. (45–60 cm), including 7–12 in. (17–30 cm) tail; 1–2.5 lbs (0.5–1.1 kg).

Diet: Nuts, twigs, buds, and tender leaves of trees; fruit; birdseed; bird eggs; nestlings.

Habitat: Wooded areas in cities and towns, along streams and rivers, and around farms and ranches.

Where to watch: Eastern Colorado into foothills of Front Range.

Abert's Squirrel
Sciurus aberti

What feature tells you that you are looking at an Abert's squirrel? Those "paintbrushes" attached to its ears. Scientists aren't sure what those crazy tufts of fur are for. Do you have any ideas?

Abert's squirrels, also called tassel-eared squirrels, depend on the ponderosa pine tree for food and shelter. If you find a pile of broken pinecones, gnawed twigs, and clipped-off pine needles beneath a ponderosa pine, look up. Is there an Abert's squirrel sitting on a branch above you, eating a pinecone for lunch?

Abert's squirrels are usually solitary, but in spring, their ponderosa pine forests get very busy. Abert's squirrels run up and down trees, chasing each other. Groups of males follow one female around, hoping she will mate with them. Usually you can't tell the boys from the girls because they look alike. At this time of year, however, the squirrels' behavior will help you know which are which.

Just the Facts

Description: Fur jet black, salt-and-pepper gray, gray with white underside and black stripes on sides, or brown; tufted ears; bushy tail; 17.5–23 in. (44–58 cm), including 8–12 in. (20–30 cm) tail; 1.2–1.6 lbs (0.5–0.7 kg).
Diet: Seeds, cones, twigs, bark, and buds of ponderosa pines.
Habitat: Ponderosa pine forests.
Where to watch: Foothills and mountains of central and southern Colorado.

(Bottom left) Most Abert's squirrels along the Front Range are jet black.
(Bottom right) Those in southwestern Colorado are salt-and-pepper gray.
(Top right) Predators would have a hard time getting past the porcupine's protective quills.

Common Porcupine
Erethizon dorsatum

How do you hug a porcupine? That's one question you don't want to answer by trial and error! The porcupine's sharp quills are actually hairs that have evolved to help protect the porcupine. What happens if a predator tries to pounce on and eat a porcupine? Ouch!

Despite their large size, porcupines are good at climbing trees. They don't have good eyesight, and they move slowly. Although they are usually nocturnal, you may spot one trundling along the floor of a mountain forest. Why are speed and good vision not important for porcupines?

If a porcupine is threatened, it hunches its back so its quills bristle outward. Have you heard that a porcupine can throw its quills? That isn't true. You're safe near a porcupine as long as you don't try to pet it!

Just the Facts

Description: Large, reddish brown, stocky body; short, thick tail; short legs; sharp quills and coarse hairs giving white or yellow wash to coat; 25–36.5 in. (64–93 cm), including 6–12 in. (15–30 cm) tail; 9–40 lbs (4–18 kg).

Diet: Inner bark, buds, leaves, or needles of trees and shrubs; grasses; flowering plants.

Habitat: Foothills, coniferous forests, cottonwood-willow woodlands, aspen groves.

Where to watch: Statewide, though most common in central and western Colorado.

Cottontails

These rabbits with the fluffy white tails are not only cute, they also play an important role in their ecosystems. They provide food for lots of different predators, including owls, coyotes, and hawks. If some female rabbits have more than fifty young in a year, why isn't Colorado overrun with rabbits?

There are actually three species of cottontails in Colorado. They look so much alike you can't easily tell which species you're looking at. The best clue is knowing where you are and which cottontail is most likely to live there. The **eastern cottontail** (*Sylvilagus floridanus*) lives mainly in the northeast part of the state, in the Platte River Valley. The **desert cottontail** (*Sylvilagus audubonii*) lives in eastern, southern, and far western Colorado, up to about 7,000 feet (2,134 m). **Mountain cottontails** (*Sylvilagus nuttallii*) inhabit the state from the Front Range foothills west to Utah. Together these three cottontails cover the state from border to border.

Just the Facts

Description: Soft, gray coat flecked with black; medium-length ears; large hind feet; fluffy tail, like a puff of cotton; 15–19 in. (38–48 cm); 1–3 lbs (0.5–1.4 kg).
Diet: Grass; wildflowers; green plants; buds, bark, twigs, and shoots of shrubs and trees (particularly in winter).
Habitat: Grasslands, shrublands, open forests.
Where to watch: Statewide.

(Above) Cottontails have shorter ears than jackrabbits and other hares.
(Right) The jackrabbit's huge ears don't miss many sounds.

Black-tailed Jackrabbit

Lepus californicus

Lots of animals eat jackrabbits, even though jackrabbits aren't the easiest prey to catch. Have you ever seen a jackrabbit run? Not only is it fast, but it zigzags. Why would this be useful for a jackrabbit escaping a predator?

Even though it is called a jackrabbit, this animal is actually a hare. What's the difference between hares and rabbits? Check "Just the Facts" for both cottontails and the jackrabbit and look at the photographs for clues. Which is bigger? Which has longer ears? Rabbit babies are born without fur and unable to see. Young hares are born with fur and their eyes open. Unlike rabbits, hares don't dig burrows for shelter. Instead they hide in little depressions beneath shrubs and tall vegetation.

Like cottontails, jackrabbits are very important as food for predators, such as coyotes and golden eagles. A female jackrabbit may have as many as thirty babies a year so that enough of her young will survive to have babies of their own.

Just the Facts

Description: Grayish black body with white underparts; black stripe on top of tail; long legs; long ears; bulging eyes; 18.5–25 in. (47–63 cm); 3–7 lbs (1.4–3.2 kg).

Diet: Grasses, sedges, wildflowers, shrubs.

Habitat: Grasslands, pastures, meadows and shrublands below 7,000 ft (2,134 m).

Where to watch: Eastern Colorado from the Front Range to Kansas; far western Colorado.

On the Trail

Maybe we should call the jackrabbit "Bigfoot." A jackrabbit's hind foot is six inches (15 cm) long. Use a ruler to measure the length of your foot from heel to toe. How do your feet compare to the jackrabbit's? Remember, the jackrabbit is only about twenty inches (51 cm) long and weighs about five pounds (2.3 kg). How tall are you and how much do you weigh?

Pika
Ochotona princeps

Imagine if you lived on a mountaintop in winter. How would you survive? The pika has an answer. This little animal lives on the roof of Colorado, above timberline. It doesn't hibernate, like some animals, but stays active all winter. The pika makes a snug den among the rocks on a rocky mountainside. Snow covers the rocks like a blanket, insulating the den and keeping the temperature above freezing. What does the pika eat? All summer the pika cuts and stores green plants, creating a "pantry" in its den. It even turns the drying plants so they cure properly, like a farmer turns his hay so it won't mold. Though these "rock farmers" have short ears and look like rodents, they are actually cousins of rabbits and hares.

If you hike above timberline in summer, you might have trouble spotting the well-camouflaged pika. But listen! That high-pitched bark you hear— *Chirk! Chirk!*—is a pika. It's scolding you for walking through its territory.

Just the Facts

Description: Small, grayish brown body; short, rounded ears; no tail; 6.5–8.5 in. (16.5–21.5 cm); 4–9 oz (120–250 g).

Diet: Leaves and stems of shrubs, wildflowers, and grass; some needles and bark of trees and shrubs.

Habitat: Rocky talus slopes above timberline and in open subalpine forests.

Where to watch: Timberline areas throughout the higher mountains of the state, above 10,000 feet (3,048 m).

(Above) Pikas store enough dried plants in their den to fill a bathtub.

Yellow-bellied Marmot
Marmota flaviventris

Whee-ooh! Whee-ooh! What makes that whistling sound you sometimes hear when you're hiking high up in the mountains? It's a whistle-pig, another name for the marmot. Marmots are related to groundhogs, although marmots aren't out on February 2 looking to see their shadows. It's still too cold and snowy where they live. Instead, they are hibernating underground.

Because the mountain winters are long, marmots may spend more than half of their lives hibernating. They can hibernate for eight months of the year, depending on conditions. Marmots dig burrows under rocks and logs and live in colonies with other marmots. Usually a colony is made up of a big, extended family—a dominant male with several females and their young. Whistling is the marmot's way of warning its family of danger. What other animal in this chapter lives in a colony and warns others of danger by barking?

Just the Facts

Description: Large rodent with thick, reddish brown fur; short legs; fairly long tail; 18.5–28 in. (47–68 cm); 3.5–11.5 lbs (1.6–5.2 kg).
Diet: Seeds, leaves, flowers, and stems of wildflowers and green plants.
Habitat: Alpine tundra, timberline forests, mountain meadows.
Where to watch: Front Range west across the state, usually above 8,000 feet (2,438 m).

(Left) Yellow-bellied marmots live in some of Colorado's most remote terrain.
(Below) An adult marmot and a youngster sun themselves on a rocky piece of tundra.

American Beaver

Castor canadensis

Next time you're in the bathtub or at a swimming pool, hold your hand out flat, with the palm down. Now slap the water surface. You just warned all the beavers in the area that danger is near. (Your mom or dad, on the other hand, may not appreciate that loud slap and splash!)

Imagine you're a beaver living in a pond in Colorado. What would you do if you heard another beaver slap its tail? You would dive underwater for safety. As a beaver, you're well equipped for diving and swimming. Your feet have webbing, or flaps of skin, between the toes, like swim flippers. You can pinch your nostrils shut, without using your hands, to keep out water. A special membrane, like a clear eyelid, covers your eye. It keeps dirt out of your eye underwater but still lets you see.

Are you ready to cut down trees with your teeth? A beaver uses the trees to build a dam across a stream, creating a pond behind the dam. The beaver builds its lodge, or house, in the middle of the new pond. This round pile of sticks is like a castle surrounded by a moat. What happens when the "moat" freezes over? Predators still can't reach the beaver because the door to its lodge is underwater.

A beaver starts a chain reaction when it builds a dam. A stream backs up. A pond forms. A meadow floods. Water-loving plants start growing where there were grass and trees. With different plants, some animals can no longer live in the changed place, but animals that like the changes move in.

Just the Facts

Description: Large, dark brown body; short ears; wide, flat tail; 2–4 ft (0.6–1.2 m), including 8–14 in. (20–35 cm) tail; 35–70 lbs (16–32 kg).

Diet: Bark, buds, leaves, and twigs of trees, such as willows, cottonwoods, and aspen.

Habitat: Mountain streams, prairie creeks, ponds, canals, reservoirs.

Where to watch: Statewide.

On the Trail

A beaver practically leaves a sign saying, "I was here!" when it cuts down a tree— if you know how to read its message. Look for pointy chiseled stumps of trees along a stream. You can see grooves in the wood from the beaver's teeth.

(Left) You can tell an active beaver pond by its well-maintained dam.
(Above) A swimming beaver leaves a V-shaped wake, like a boat.
(Below) Beavers store tender tree limbs underwater for winter food.

Winging from

B irds, birds—what would Colorado be without birds? There are birds all over our state and everywhere we turn. Some live on the open prairie. Others live near people in parks and backyards. Lots of birds live in mountain forests and meadows, especially in summer. Some even live at the top of Colorado's mountains, on the alpine tundra.

Not all birds are here year-round. Imagine you're a bird that eats insects for a living. Are there many insects around in winter? You would have a tough time finding food. A good rule of thumb is that bug-eaters migrate here in the spring, then head south again in winter. Birds that eat seeds, nuts, and berries can stay here all year long. Even most of those move to lower elevations where the winters are not so harsh.

Do you know how to identify birds? Look and listen. Birds come in different shapes, colors, and sizes. They live in different habitats. Notice where you see certain birds. Compare the shape of their beaks, their size, how they act. Listen to their songs. If you pay attention, the birds will tell you about themselves.

Steller's jay

Black-billed magpie

Lark bunting

Prairie to Peak

Western meadowlark

Mountain bluebird

White-tailed ptarmigan

Wild turkey

Broad-tailed hummingbirds

House finch

Western Meadowlark
Sturnella neglecta

If you could make sunshine into music, it would surely come out as the bright song of the western meadowlark. The meadowlark is a bird of prairies and open country, where its song dances across the grass.

Meadowlarks differ from many other songbirds in that they don't migrate. They stay here in Colorado year-round. When their main food, insects, disappears, they live on grass and weed seeds. In winter, when the meadowlark is silent, you can still recognize it. Watch when a meadowlark flies. Notice how it flutters with busy wingbeats, then glides with its wings stretched out. You will also see the flash of the white edges on its tail. These clues tell us the meadowlark's identity, even when it seems to blend into the drab winter prairie.

To pioneer children whose families settled in eastern Colorado, the meadowlark was a cheery neighbor. To them his bright song proclaimed, "Gee-whiz-whillikers!" Other people are sure the meadowlark is singing, "Yes, I am a pretty little bird." What does the meadowlark's song say to you?

People tend to think of the meadowlark as a prairie bird, but it actually lives in open grassy areas all across the state, including mountain parks. If you were a bird living in a land with no trees, where would you build your nest? On the ground, of course, carefully hidden among the grass and shrubs. The female meadowlark builds her nest of dried grasses with a domed roof, and a doorway on the side. She sneaks secretly into her nest so she won't lead predators to her chicks.

Just the Facts

Description: Medium-size songbird; gray-brown feathers speckled with black; bright yellow breast; black V on chest; about 9.5 in. (24 cm) from beak to tail.

Diet: Insects, grass, weed seeds.

Habitat: Prairies, farm fields, pastures, mountain grasslands and meadows, sometimes in western shrublands.

Where to watch: Eastern Colorado; also statewide in suitable habitat.

On the Trail

Watch for singing western meadowlarks perched atop yucca stalks or fence posts. The male meadowlark's open beak makes a V against the sky. Notice how it matches the black V on his bright yellow breast. Unlike many songbirds, female and male meadowlarks look alike, but only the male sings. He makes music to proclaim his territory and attract a mate.

(Above) Meadowlarks eat insects in summer and switch to seeds for winter.
(Right) Like many birds, meadowlarks get water from puddles.
(Left) A male meadowlark sings from a perch.

Black-billed Magpie
Pica pica

Doesn't this common Colorado bird look like it's parading around in a tuxedo? It makes quite a sight trailing that long tail. In some light the magpie's black feathers glow purple and green. Bird-watchers from the eastern United States come here especially to see this western bird.

The magpie's bold behavior and hoarse voice may remind you of its cousins, the crows and jays. Birds in the crow family are known for their adaptability, intelligence, and for not being shy. Magpies will even hop past a sleeping dog to steal food from its bowl. Because they eat a wide variety of food, magpies can live here year-round. Like most jays and crows, male and female magpies look alike.

You have probably seen magpie nests in trees many times. They build a jumble of sticks with an interesting feature. Their nests have a roof over them! There are entrances on both sides. Sometimes you can look right through a magpie's nest.

Just the Facts

Description: Large bird; bold black-and-white plumage; strong black bill; long tail; 19 in. (48 cm) from beak to tail.

Diet: Insects, carrion, small mammals, seeds, fruit, garbage.

Habitat: Stands of trees or shrubs in open country; farmland, pastures, shrublands; urban areas.

Where to watch: Statewide.

(Top left) The magpie's black plumage shines green and purple in the sun.
(Top right) Magpies often gather in large groups, especially around food.

Lark Bunting

Calamospiza melanocorys

Some people question why the lark bunting, a prairie bird, is Colorado's state bird, but look at a state map. Draw an imaginary line through Fort Collins, Denver, and Pueblo. All the land east of this line, almost half our state, is prairie grassland.

If you drive on country roads in eastern Colorado in summer, you might see lark buntings sitting on fence posts. The males are very handsome, all black with white patches on the shoulders. The females are harder to identify. They're a streaky brown. But when they fly, you can see the white patches on their brown wings, looking like a drab version of the male.

Did you notice any male lark buntings "dancing" in the air? They're performing their courtship song flight, called skylarking. The male flies up in the sky, then spirals slowly down like a butterfly, singing away. Most songbirds perch in a tree to sing. Why would a song flight make sense for a prairie bird?

(Far right) This male lark bunting sits atop a thistle.
(Right) The female's plumage is less striking than the male's.

Backyard Birds

There's a little brown bird with a bright red head and throat that is very common in Colorado backyards. It's called a **house finch** (*Carpodacus mexicanus*). The male has the red coloring. The female is a streaky brown. In spring, you might hear a male house finch singing a cheery, bubbly song that seems to go on and on. House finches often build their nests around houses—under the eaves of a roof, in backyard shrubs, even in hanging plants.

If you've ever watched crows, you know they aren't shy. **American crows** (*Corvus brachyrhynchos*) adapt well to life around people. They've learned to help themselves to spilled dog food, French fries, and all sorts of garbage. In fact, crows have been slowly spreading across Colorado, even up into the mountains. They often hang out in groups with other crows, sort of like teenagers at a mall. The crow's call is not a pretty sound—*Caw! Caw!*— but these birds do seem to have an opinion.

The **black-capped chickadee** (*Poecile atricapillus*) is one of those birds named for its call. It calls out in a buzzy voice, *Tsik-a-dee-dee*. Maybe you've heard a chickadee singing, *Fee-bee*. The song goes down on the *bee* part.

(Bottom) House finches, such as this male, are one of the most common birds seen at feeders.
(Below) American crows are growing in number across the state.
(Right) The energetic black-capped chickadee visits lots of bird feeders in winter.
(Far right) Is your backyard home to a northern flicker, with a black crescent on its breast?

Try whistling back a *Fee-bee* when you hear it. The chickadee will probably answer you.

Chickadees are quite small but very busy and lively. They are common in Colorado backyards, especially in winter. In summer many of them move up into mountain forests, where they nest.

Have you ever heard a loud *Chuk! Chuk! Chuk!* sound in your neighborhood in spring? Listen also for a loud tapping—*Ta-ta-ta-tat*. What's making all that racket? Your backyard woodpecker, the **northern flicker** *(Colaptes auratus),* is announcing its territory. Watch for the flash of the flicker's white rump and the reddish lining of its wings when it flies. Flickers' favorite food is ants. That's why you often see them on the ground poking in the dirt with their beaks.

Steller's Jay
Cyanocitta stelleri

Want to speak the Steller's jay's language? In a hoarse voice, shout *Shak-shak-shak!* If you really want to be a jay, tie a pointy black crest on your head. Now fly into the branches of a pine tree, and peer down at a family picnicking below. Hop around branch-to-branch for a closer look. Steller's jays have learned they can pick up tidbits at mountain picnic grounds. Just remember not to feed them. People food isn't healthy for wild animals.

You may be familiar with eastern blue jays. How do they differ from Steller's jays? Steller's jays are native to Colorado's mountains. Blue jays had never been seen here until 1903. They moved into our state because of changes humans made to the land. Now in some places, blue jays are competing with Steller's jays for habitat.

Just the Facts

Description: Deep, gleaming blue body; black head and crest; white streaks on forehead; white eyebrows; 11.5 in. (29 cm) from beak to tail.

Diet: Seeds, pine nuts, insects, berries, small birds and eggs, toads.

Habitat: Coniferous forests, especially of ponderosa pine; piñon-juniper woodlands.

Where to watch: Foothills and mountains from the Front Range west across the state.

Mountain Bluebird
Sialia currucoides

To hunt for insects on the ground, mountain bluebirds hover in place like helicopters. When a bluebird spots a grasshopper, it drops down and snaps it up. Western bluebirds, cousins of mountain bluebirds, often watch for insects by sitting on top of a low tree. Mountain bluebirds, however, live in mountain meadows and pastures. Why would hovering make sense for them?

Although bluebirds are bug-eaters, many stay in Colorado for the winter, moving to lower elevations. They change their diet to seeds and berries. They will even visit bird feeders for seeds, raisins, and peanut butter.

Is a bluebird always blue? It often looks dull and gray when the light is poor. The bluebird's color doesn't come from pigment. It's produced by light reflecting and refracting (bending) off of tiny spines on the feathers. The feathers absorb all the colors except blue. Blue light is reflected back to our eyes. That's why we see the bluebird as blue.

(Far right) Bluebirds nest in cavities, or holes, in trees and will readily use human-made nest boxes.
(Right) Bluebirds feast on insects in summer.
(Left) Steller's jays nest in mountain pine forests and show up at bird feeders at lower elevations in the winter.

Just the Facts

Description: Male: sky blue feathers, paler breast. Female: gray feathers with blue wash on wings and tail. Both: 7 in. (18 cm) from beak to tail.
Diet: Insects, seeds, berries.
Habitat: Mountain meadows; pastures and shrublands near open woodlands, especially piñon-juniper and ponderosa pine woodlands.
Where to watch: Foothills of the Front Range west across the state, spring through fall. Southern and southwestern Colorado, winter.

Wild Turkey
Meleagris gallopavo

Take twenty birds the size of suitcases. Paint them greenish brown. Stick them up in the very tops of trees, where they look way too big to sit. Now you have a roosting flock of wild turkeys. Turkeys spend most of their waking hours on the ground poking around for food. They are quite heavy for the size of their wings, so they don't fly very well. They can fly well enough to flutter up into treetops for the night, safe from predators. In spring the males attract mates by fanning their tails, strutting around, and gobbling.

Do you eat turkey for Thanksgiving? The turkey on your table came from a farm, but its ancestors, hundreds of years ago, were wild turkeys from the Americas. When the Spanish colonized Mexico, they took turkeys back to Europe with them. Then European settlers brought turkeys back to North America as farm animals.

Just the Facts

Description: Metallic bronze feathers with green, gold, and red reflections; full tail; naked red, purple, or blue head and neck; 37–46 in. (94–117 cm) from beak to tail. Male: nearly 4 ft (1.2 m) tall; 20–25 lbs (9–11 kg).

Diet: Acorns, seeds, insects, frogs, lizards, mice.

Habitat: Ponderosa pine forests with an understory of oak brush; riparian areas.

Where to watch: Southern Colorado; along Arkansas and South Platte Rivers.

White-tailed Ptarmigan
Lagopus leucurus

Do birds change their clothes? The white-tailed ptarmigan does. In fall it sheds its brown summer feathers and grows a new set of all-white ones. Why? Ptarmigans live high on the alpine tundra. In winter lots of snow covers the land. Could the ptarmigan hide from predators if it were still brown? When spring comes, the ptarmigan grows a new set of speckled brown-and-white feathers so that it will blend in with the rocks. The ptarmigan changes its plumage twice a year to match its habitat.

In fall, lots of birds migrate south. Others move from the high mountains to lower elevations. The ptarmigan toughs it out on top of the state's highest mountains—without hibernating. Ptarmigans huddle together in the shelter of alpine willows. Snow insulates them from the cold like a blanket. Did you know ptarmigans wear "snowshoes?" Feathers on their feet help them walk on deep snow without sinking.

Just the Facts

Description: Feathers white in winter, mottled brown-and-white in summer, and somewhere in-between in spring and fall; 12.5 in. (32 cm) from beak to tail.

Diet: Buds, flowers, and twigs of alpine willows and other alpine plants.

Habitat: Willow thickets of alpine tundra.

Where to watch: Mount Evans, Guanella Pass, Trail Ridge Road in Rocky Mountain National Park, Cottonwood Pass, Independence Pass.

*Can you spot the ptarmigan in these pictures? A ptarmigan's plumage changes with the seasons— from summer **(far right)** to fall **(middle right)** to winter **(right)**.*
*(**Top left**) Male turkeys fan their handsome tails to impress females.*
*(**Top right**) Wild turkeys look like overgrown songbirds when they roost in trees.*

Broad-tailed Hummingbird
Selasphorus platycercus

Like a shrill, green bullet, a hummingbird whizzes past your head. Did you hear the whistling hum of his wings? When a male broad-tailed hummingbird flaps his wings, air passes through slots between the feathers. It creates a humming sound, like blowing on a kazoo. That whistling buzz is the way the male hummingbird lets other birds know he is coming and they had better look out!

Hummingbirds are like bird stunt pilots. They can fly forward and backward and hover in place like a helicopter. They can even fly upside down, for a very brief time. Ever wonder how a hummingbird hovers in the air? Hold your arms out to the sides with your palms up. Now turn your hands over and then back up, making a figure eight in the air. Do this fifty times in a second. That's how fast a hummingbird moves its wings when it hovers! The hummer's wings flap so fast, they look like a blur.

In some countries hummingbirds are called flower-kissers because they slip their bills into flowers. Nectar inside flowers is the humming-bird's main food. The sugary nectar is good food for hummingbirds because they use up lots of energy. Hummingbirds also catch insects. Insects give them protein in their diet. Considering what they eat, why do hummingbirds have to leave Colorado when summer is over?

There are more than 300 kinds of hummingbirds in the Americas, but only three species show up regularly in Colorado. You are most likely to see the broad-tailed hummingbird. The birds will come readily to a nectar feeder filled with one part sugar and four parts boiled water.

Just the Facts

Description: Male: iridescent green back and wings; whitish undersides; throat magenta-red in light. Female: iridescent green with buffy, faintly streaked undersides. Both: 4 in. (10 cm) from beak to tail.
Diet: Flower nectar, tree sap, insects.
Habitat: Mountain forests, meadows, and riparian areas.
Where to watch: Front Range west across the state, spring through fall. Eastern Plains during migration, late April and late September.

(Right) *A hummingbird hovers like a helicopter while drinking nectar from a flower.* **(Below)** *The bright red throat tells you this is a male broad-tailed hummingbird.*

On the Trail

Hummingbirds are active from dawn until dusk. Look for them in willow thickets along mountain streams or in mountain meadows where wildflowers are blooming. Sometimes you hear a hummingbird before you see it.

Water-Lovers

Some birds are more at home in or near the water than in the air. We see these water-lovers throughout Colorado—in city parks, on farm ponds, along streams, and on lakes. Some of them, such as ducks and their bigger cousins, geese, have webbed feet. Why is this a good adaptation for living on water?

When you go out in the rain, you put on a raincoat to stay dry. The feathers of ducks and geese act like a raincoat. Imagine swimming and diving all day long and never getting your skin wet! That's how effective geese and ducks' waterproof feathers are. Though pelicans aren't ducks or geese, they swim a lot, too. Would it make sense for them to have waterproof feathers and webbed feet?

Some water-loving birds just wade in the water to gather food. They look very different from ducks and geese. They have long legs, necks, and bills. If you're sitting high up on long legs, it helps to have a long neck so you can reach down to the ground for food. Since they wade instead of swimming, do you suppose wading birds have webbed feet? Read on to find out!

Canada goose

American avocet

with Wings

Ducks

Great blue heron

American white pelicans

American coots

Mallards

Sandhill cranes

On the Trail

When you see Canada geese in a park, they may not seem to notice you. But if you walk toward them, one or two of the geese may start honking. Some of the geese in a flock are always watchful. These sentries alert the other geese to danger. Watch how they lower and straighten their long necks and hiss to challenge a stranger.

Canada Goose
Branta canadensis

Do you want to learn to speak "goose"? First you need a friend to help you. One of you say *Hah!* Then the other one answer a note higher, *onk!* Repeat this several times—*Hah-onk! Hah-onk!* Now, if the two of you could fly while honking, you'd really make good geese! When a pair of Canada geese are flying, they "talk" to each other. The first one starts the honk, and its mate answers with the rest of the honk. Listen when geese fly over. Can you hear the two parts of their honk? If you were busy flying and wanted to be sure your partner was nearby, wouldn't this be a good way to keep in touch?

In spring mother and father geese swim with their fluffy black-and-yellow babies trailing along like a string of beads. When young birds of most species are grown up, they leave their parents, but young geese stay with their parents for a year. They migrate together with other families of geese.

Lots of Canada geese live in Colorado. Some stay here year-round. Lots more come here in the winter, especially to cities and suburbs along the Front Range. Why would they stop in Colorado instead of migrating farther south? Canada geese eat grass. What do you see everywhere around a city? Grass—on people's lawns, in city parks, on golf courses. The geese see that green grass, too, and they fly down for a meal. Plus, there are lots of ponds and lakes where they can find open water, even in winter.

Just the Facts

Description: Large, grayish brown body; black bill and head; long black neck with white "chinstrap"; 25–45 in. (64–114 cm) from bill to tail.

Diet: Grass; corn and other grains left in farm fields after harvest; algae; aquatic plants.

Habitat: Ponds, lakes, canals, and streams; marshes and wet meadows; grassy banks of waterways; parks, golf courses, farm fields.

Where to watch: Eastern Colorado, year-round. Mountain parks and valleys, summer. Statewide during migration.

(Top) How many goslings, or baby geese, do you count in this family?

(Middle) Canada geese save energy by flying in groups. The lead goose "breaks through" the air, so the geese behind it don't have to work as hard.

(Bottom) This goose's stretched-out neck and open bill are a warning to keep your distance.

Mallard
Anas platyrhynchos

The emerald green head of the mallard drake (male duck) glows in the sun. The drab brown duck swimming beside him is a mallard, too—a female. Many female birds are dull and not brightly colored. The female mallard sits on the eggs and protects her young ducklings. What might happen if she were colorful and easy to spot?

If you watch mallard drakes in spring, they seem to flutter and splash a lot. The drake lifts his breast and tail out of the water and flares his wings. Sometimes the male whistles, squirts water at a female, and shakes his tail and head. These displays are how a drake tries to attract a mate.

Mallards are dabbling ducks. They float on the water and tip bottoms-up to reach food underwater. The female mallard does all the quacking. She gives a loud *Quak, quak-quak-quak*, that goes down in pitch. The male gives a hoarse *Reb-reb*.

Just the Facts

Description: Large duck; 23 in. (58 cm) from bill to tail. Male: shiny green head, grayish body, yellow bill. Female: mottled brown.
Diet: Aquatic plants, algae, grain, seeds, insects.
Habitat: Open freshwater ponds, lakes, streams, canals; suburban parks and gardens.
Where to watch: Statewide, year-round.

(Above) As with many duck species, the female mallard raises the ducklings by herself.
(Right) The mallard drake's gleaming green head is a sure clue for identifying him.

Other Water Birds

Hooded mergansers *(Lophodytes cucullatus)* have thinner bills than most ducks. When he's excited, the male hooded merganser can raise the feathers of his head crest like a big fan. Watch for mergansers along rivers and streams of eastern Colorado, especially in winter, and in western Colorado valleys and mountain parks.

Can ducks perch in trees? **Wood ducks** *(Aix sponsa)* can. They nest in holes in trees. When the ducklings leave the nest, they flutter and tumble to the ground and then walk to water. Look for wood ducks along tree-lined riparian areas in eastern Colorado and western Colorado's Grand Valley.

The **American coot** *(Fulica americana)* looks like a duck, but it's not. Instead of webbed feet, it has flaps of skin on its toes to help it paddle. The coot's nickname is mudhen. Coots squabble and squawk like chickens, and their bills are more like a chicken's than a duck's.

(Top) The male hooded merganser fans his head crest when he's agitated. *(Above left)* The male wood duck is one of the most colorful of all ducks. *(Below)* Together a male and female American coot build a floating nest anchored among the cattails.

American White Pelican

Pelecanus erythrorhynchos

"What a wonderful bird is the pelican. His bill will hold more than his *belican*." This line from a limerick by Dixon Merritt isn't far from the truth. The pelican's bill has a big pouch of stretchy skin attached to the lower jaw. That pouch is like the net you use to catch fish in an aquarium. That's exactly how a pelican uses it, too. The bird sits on the surface of a shallow lake or pond, dips its bill down into the water, and scoops up fish. It quickly closes its mouth so the fish won't wriggle out. Then the bird squeezes the water out of the pouch and swallows the fish whole—*gulp*. The explorers Lewis and Clark caught a pelican and measured how much water it could hold in its pouch. Can you guess the amount? Five gallons. That's enough water to fill a kitchen sink!

Pelicans often fish as a team. A group of them lines up side-by-side on the water. Then they slowly paddle toward shallow water. Sometimes they get in a circle and swim toward each other. They aren't just playing around. The pelicans are working together to herd fish into a small space where the birds can catch them. There's a lot of splashing as the pelicans suddenly gobble up the fish.

Have you seen groups of pelicans flying together? Sometimes flying pelicans look like a formation of air force jets. If the first bird makes a slow turn, each one in line follows on the same flight pattern. By flying exactly behind another bird, each pelican saves wing-flapping energy.

Just the Facts

Description: Very large, white bird; short legs; long, orange bill; black wing tips; 62 in. (158 cm) from bill to tail; 9 ft (2.7 m) wingspan.

Diet: Fish.

Habitat: Relatively large, shallow ponds and lakes.

Where to watch: Eastern Colorado, North Park, South Park, larger mountain lakes, spring through fall.

(Above) Pelican hatchlings eat food their parents carry in their stomachs and spit up.
(Top and middle right) Can't you almost hear the splashing and gobbling as these pelicans work together to catch fish?
(Bottom) White pelicans' broad wings have black wing tips.

On the Trail

If you stood at the edge of a lake in eastern Colorado, a pelican might fly in for a landing right over your head. You could easily think a small aircraft had just flown over! That's because a pelican's wings stretch nine feet from tip to tip.

American Avocet
Recurvirostra americana

Take a crow-size bird. Set it up on stilts. Now take a straw, bend it up in the middle, and glue it on the bird's face for a bill. Paint the bird with big splashes of black and white. Then paint its neck and head orange. You have made an avocet.

Why would long, skinny legs and a long, up-curving bill be useful? Avocets wade through shallow water, sweeping their bills back and forth underwater. That up-curved bill lets them feel prey in the water. No other bird in North America has a bill quite like the avocet's.

In winter, avocets live in southern California and Mexico, and their orange heads turn gray. When spring comes and it's time to look flashy to attract a mate, they lose the gray head feathers and grow new, bright orange ones.

Just the Facts

Description: Black-and-white body and wings; orange head and long, slender neck; long, up-curved bill; long, thin, blue legs; 18 in. (46 cm) from bill to tail.

Diet: Insects, crayfish, small fish, seeds.

Habitat: Marshy shorelines of ponds and lakes, flooded fields, temporary pools along country roads.

Where to watch: Eastern Colorado, North Park, San Luis Valley, spring through fall.

(Above) Long legs help the avocet step quietly in the water.

Sandhill Crane
Grus canadensis

Have you ever been on a car trip with your family and stopped to eat lunch, buy gas, and stretch your legs? Each March, as many as 20,000 sandhill cranes stop in the San Luis Valley in southern Colorado to do essentially the same thing. They are on a long migration flight to their nesting grounds, and this valley's fields and meadows are a good place to rest and refuel. Some of the cranes are headed for northwestern Colorado.

Listen. Do you hear a wonderful, musical call rising from the fields? *Ka-rooo, ka-rooo* That's the song of the cranes. Watch as they bow and leap and prance. Through song and dance, male and female cranes tell each other that they are ready to nest and raise young cranes. In spring and fall, you may see and hear cranes migrating high overhead, particularly along the east side of the Front Range.

Just the Facts

Description: Tall with gray body; often rusty colored because of mud stains; long legs and neck; red patch on head; 3.5–4 ft (1.1–1.2 m) tall; 3.5 ft (1.1 m) from bill to tail.
Diet: Seeds, roots, berries, grain left in fields after harvest, frogs, mice, snails, insects.
Habitat: Marshes; wet meadows; shallow rivers, ponds, and lakes.
Where to watch: San Luis Valley, March; Yampa River and northwestern Colorado, spring through fall.

(Top) Sandhill cranes dance to demonstrate their attachment to their mates.
(Far left) Sandhill cranes migrate by the thousands through Colorado each spring.
(Left) This baby sandhill crane doesn't have its parent's long legs yet, but it can run soon after hatching.

On the Trail

Great blue herons and sandhill cranes look a lot alike—long necks, long skinny legs, blue-gray feathers. Here's a trick to tell them apart when they're flying. Cranes fly with their long necks stretched out. Herons fly with their necks curved back in an S. Also, only herons can perch in trees. A crane's three toes can't grab a tree branch and hold on. A heron's four toes—with one pointing backward—can.

(Above) Great blue herons fly with their long legs extended and their necks folded.
(Below) Herons grab or spear prey with their long bills.
(Right) Male and female great blue herons look alike.

Great Blue Heron

Ardea herodias

Have you ever seen a tall, blue-gray bird poised at the edge of a pond or stream? Did it stand so still you thought it was sleeping? Don't be fooled. That bird was a great blue heron, and it was really quite busy. Great blue herons stand incredibly still so they don't ripple the water and scare away a likely meal. The heron is watching for prey. Its eyes are like binoculars. They can focus through the water. When the heron spots a tasty morsel—zap!—it grabs a frog or fish fast as lightning with its long, pointy bill.

Watch how a heron walks oh-so-slowly through the water. It lifts one leg up until its foot is out of the water. Then it steps very carefully. Next time you're in a pool or a lake, try walking like a heron. Can you move without splashing or rippling the water? With such long, slender legs, a heron can walk and stand in the water, and prey animals won't know it's there.

Herons nest in colonies with other herons. Their big nests look like jumbles of sticks built way up high in the branches of trees along lakes and streams. Herons are big birds, with very wide wings. Watching them, you may wonder how the long-legged adults will ever fold those big wings and land in the trees without crashing. Some herons migrate, but others stay in Colorado year-round. As long as there is open, unfrozen water, the herons can find food and don't need to spend energy migrating.

Just the Facts

Description: Large, gray-blue body; long legs and neck; spearlike bill; long, feathery plume of black feathers on back of head during breeding season; 3.5 ft (1.1 m) tall; 46 in. (117 cm) from bill to tail.

Diet: Small fish, crayfish, insects, frogs, snakes, mice.

Habitat: Marshes, edges of ponds and lakes, streams.

Where to watch: Eastern Colorado, year-round; mountain parks and valleys, summer.

Canada lynx

Gray wolves

Black-footed ferret

Colorado Critters in Danger

Some of the animals covered in this book are endangered or threatened. *Endangered* means that a species has become so rare that it is in danger of becoming extinct, vanishing completely from the earth. A threatened species is one whose numbers are getting smaller. It could become endangered unless it gets help and protection.

How does this happen? When people move onto land where wildlife lives, they usually change or destroy the animals' habitat. Some animals cannot adjust to new habitat, and they die. People also often destroy wildlife that might kill their livestock, or that lives on land where they want to build a house, farm, ranch, or subdivision. If enough animals of one species die, the species can become threatened or endangered.

Some animals have already disappeared from our state. Millions of bison once inhabited Colorado. Hunters killed so many that bison are no longer wild here. Now they live only as captive animals in parks or on ranches. Wolves and grizzly bears once roamed Colorado's prairies and mountains. Because they sometimes killed cattle and sheep and people feared them, they were trapped, poisoned, and shot. Neither wolves nor grizzly bears have been seen in Colorado for decades.

Black-footed ferrets, cousins to weasels, used to live in prairie dog towns. The ferrets died out as prairie dogs were killed off to make room for farms and ranches. Now there are plans to bring back ferrets and release them into the wild in northwestern Colorado.

For many years biologists weren't sure if any lynx still survived in Colorado. Now this shy cat, a close cousin of the bobcat, is making a comeback in our state. In 1999, the Colorado Division of Wildlife began releasing these wild cats into the remote central mountains.

Did you read about the bald eagle and peregrine falcon in "Hunters from the Sky"? Their success stories give us hope that we can save other endangered species. We can help endangered wildlife by protecting them and their habitat, although such efforts depend on public support. It's fun living in or visiting a state with so many wonderful animals. Let's make sure Colorado remains a good home or place to visit for wild critters, too.

Grizzly bear

Glossary

Adaptation: A certain characteristic, body part, or behavior a species has acquired over many generations that allows it to better survive in its habitat.
Aquatic: Living in water.

Bachelor herd: A group of male animals.
Biologist: A scientist who studies animals and plants.

Carcass: A dead animal's body.
Carnivore: An animal that eats meat. Also, a member of a group of mammals that have teeth adapted to cutting and tearing flesh.
Carrion: The remains of a dead animal.
Coniferous: Made up of conifers. A conifer is a tree, such as a pine or spruce, that has needles instead of leaves and bears its seeds on the scales of cones.
Courtship: Ways animals act during the mating season to attract mates. Courtship behavior is acted out in the same way by all animals of one species.

DDT: A pesticide that thinned the eggshells of many raptors, causing the eggs to break before the young could hatch. DDT's use was banned in 1972.

Ecosystem: A system in nature made up of plants, animals, landscape features, water, and natural processes such as weather, all of which constantly affect and change each other.
Endangered: A species that has become so rare that it is in danger of becoming extinct.
Evolved: Changed over many generations.
Extinct: When all animals of a species die and there are no more of it left on earth.

Habitat: The place where an animal lives, which provides the animal with the food, water, shelter, and living space it needs to survive.
Hibernation: An animal's resting state during the winter.

Metabolism: A body's chemical processes, such as breathing oxygen or digesting food, that allow an animal to live and use energy.

Migration: The movement of animals from one place to another, usually for feeding or breeding.

Nocturnal: Active at night.

Plumage: A bird's coat of feathers.
Predator: An animal that hunts other animals for food.
Prey: An animal that is hunted by other animals.

Raptor: A bird, such as a hawk, eagle, falcon, or owl, that uses its sharp beak and talons to catch and kill prey. Also known as a bird of prey.
Retractable: Able to be pulled back in.
Riparian: Along streams, rivers, ponds, or other bodies of water.
Rodent: A gnawing mammal with ever-growing incisors (front teeth). Also, a member of a group of mammals that includes rats, mice, beavers, and squirrels.

Species: Animals that share the same characteristics and are more like each other than like any other animal. They can mate and produce healthy young. Each species is known by a scientific name, such as *Canis latrans* for the coyote.

Talons: Sharp, curving claws on the feet of a raptor. Talons are used to catch and kill prey.
Threatened: A species whose populations are getting smaller and that could become endangered without help and protection.
Timberline: The point above which no trees can grow; the border between subalpine forests and alpine tundra.

Understory: The trees and shrubs that live between a forest's canopy and its ground cover.

Index